IF YOU LOVE BOOKS, YOU COULD BE...

By Elizabeth Dennis   Illustrated by Natalie Kwee

Ready-to-Read

SIMON SPOTLIGHT

An imprint of Simon & Schuster Children's Publishing Division
1230 Avenue of the Americas, New York, New York 10020
This Simon Spotlight edition August 2020
Text copyright © 2020 by Simon & Schuster, Inc.
Illustrations copyright © 2020 by Natalie Kwee
Manufactured in the United States of America 0720 LAK
2 4 6 8 10 9 7 5 3 1
This book has been cataloged by the Library of Congress. LCCN 2020937261
ISBN 978-1-5344-7102-3 (hc)
ISBN 978-1-5344-7101-6 (pbk)
ISBN 978-1-5344-7103-0 (eBook)

Glossary

Acquire: to buy the rights to publish a manuscript

Author: a person who writes the words in a book

Book cover: the front of a book, which includes the book's title

Book designer: a person who works on what book covers and interiors look like, sometimes with photographs or illustrations

Editor: a person who helps authors make the words and stories in their books better

Font: a set of letters, commas, periods, and other marks that are all in one style

Interior: the inside of something, such as the pages in a book

Librarian: a person who manages and takes care of a library's books and other items

Library: a place with books, computers, and other materials that people can borrow and use to get information

Manuscript: an early version of a story before it becomes a book

Publishing: preparing, printing, and selling books

Publishing house: a company that publishes books

Submission: a manuscript, or sometimes even an idea, that an editor receives from a writer and decides whether or not to publish as a book

Note to readers: Some of these words may have more than one definition. The definitions above are how these words are used in this book.

CONTENTS

Introduction

Do you love spending time
in libraries and bookstores?
Is story time your favorite
part of school?

Did you know that some people get to work with books as part of their job? When you grow up, you could too!

Chapter 1:
Editor

Do you love reading stories? Then you might want to be an editor. Editors work on a book's words and story, often at companies called publishing (say: PUB-lish-ing) houses. Publishing means preparing and printing books to be sold.

Editors work on books
for kids or adults.
They also often focus
on certain types of books,
like cookbooks or comics.

Editors choose which books
to publish by reviewing submissions
(say: sub-MISH-uns),
the story ideas that authors
hope to publish.

For example, an author's submission could include an idea for a book about soccer.
A submission can be a few sentences or a few chapters long.
It might even be a full manuscript (say: MAN-you-skript),
which is all the words in a book.

Editors read many submissions, but don't publish most of them. They look for great writing, interesting characters, and stories that feel new and fresh.

If an editor likes a submission,
they present it at a company meeting.
If other people like it too,
the editor offers to acquire
(say: uh-KWIRE),
or buy and publish, the submission.

Next, the editor and author try
to make the manuscript the best
it can be. They might change
a few words or entire chapters.

Editors must be patient and read
the same story many times.
If the book has pictures,
they also make sure the art matches
the story. They look for errors,
such as children playing soccer
with a baseball!

Editors also write book descriptions,
attend meetings to talk about
the book, and much more.

It is all worth it when they see
the finished book in bookstores!

If you want to be an editor,
the best thing you can do is to read
a lot. What kind of books
would you like to edit someday?

Chapter 2: Book Designer

What makes you pick up a book?
If it's a fun or interesting cover,
you might want to be a book designer!
Designers decide what books look like.
Some designers work on book covers
and some also work on interiors, or
the inside of a book.

For each book, they choose a font,
a set of letters and symbols
that are a certain style.
The font must be easy to read
and fit the book's topic.

A font that looks scary would not
fit a book about a nice bunny!

Designers and editors talk about
what to show on the cover
and whether to use photographs
or illustrations.
They look at many artists
before choosing one.

After the artist creates the art,
the designer puts the title
and other details into place.

Sometimes designers spend hours
looking for the perfect color
for a cover to match
the book's story. For example,
if the story happens at night,
the cover could be dark blue.

The designer brings a few choices
for the cover to a meeting.
People from all over the company
decide which one they like best.
The designer uses ideas
from the meeting to create
an even better cover.

If a book has pictures inside,
designers help decide what the artist
should show on each page.
They also put the art and words
in place and make sure it all fits.

If you want to be a book designer,
try drawing a new cover for your
favorite book. What cover would
make your friends want to read it?

Chapter 3: Librarian

If you love sharing
your favorite books with friends,
you could be a librarian.
Librarians manage the books
and other items inside libraries.
They also help people find
information in books and
on the Internet.

Librarians choose which books
to order for their library.
They also plan events like
story time, music classes,
and summer reading programs
for people who visit the library.

All libraries have books.
Some libraries also let people
borrow movies, music, games,
and even fishing rods, tools,
clothing, or seeds!

Schools and museums
have libraries and librarians too.

Companies that have
a lot of books and information
may also have librarians.

Wherever they are, librarians
work with a lot of different people.
They must be very organized.
They must also be good at
learning new information
and sharing what they learn.

If you want to be a librarian,
visit your local library.
Ask a librarian to share a
favorite book with you!

There are many kinds of jobs
for people who love reading.

Someday, you could edit, design, or work with books that people love to read!

Editor, designer, and librarian are just a few of the cool careers for people who love books. Turn the page to discover even more!

More Cool Book Careers!

An **agent** helps connect authors with editors who might want to publish their manuscripts. They also help authors with the business and legal details of publishing a book.

An **author** writes the words inside books.

A **book marketer**

comes up with ways to reach people who might want to read a book, such as by making bookmarks to give away.

A **book publicist** shares

information about books with people, newspapers, magazines, and websites to let readers know about new books.

A **bookseller** buys books from publishers to sell at a bookstore.

An **illustrator** is an artist who makes the pictures in book covers and interiors.

A **managing editor**

keeps track of schedules and due dates for books. They work with editors, designers, and production managers to make sure books go to the printer on time and without errors in spelling, punctuation, and grammar.

A **production manager**

works with printing companies to figure out how much it will cost to print books and how to make them more affordable.

A **sales representative**

sells books to bookstores, museums, and other places that offer books for sale.